KT-512-644

WARWICK
LIBRARY
SCHOOL

This book is to be returned on or before
the last date stamped below.

2 0 FEB 2006

- 9 SEP 2013

Campus Library Services Limited

51154

WARWICK SCHOOL

THE MAKING OF THE MIDDLE EAST

David Downing

www.raintreepublishers.co.uk

Visit our website to find out more information about **Raintree** books.

To order:

☎ Phone 44 (0) 1865 888112

▤ Send a fax to 44 (0) 1865 314091

▢ Visit the Raintree bookshop at **www.raintreepublishers.co.uk** to browse our catalogue and order online.

MONKEY PUZZLE MEDIA LTD

Produced for Raintree by
Monkey Puzzle Media Ltd.
Gissing's Farm, Fressingfield
Suffolk IP21 5SH, UK

First published in Great Britain by Raintree,
Halley Court, Jordan Hill, Oxford OX2 8EJ,
part of Harcourt Education.
Raintree is a registered trademark of Harcourt
Education Ltd.

© Harcourt Education Ltd 2006
The moral right of the proprietor has been asserted.

All rights reserved. No part of this publication may
be reproduced, stored in a retrieval system, or
transmitted in any form or by any means, electronic,
mechanical, photocopying, recording, or otherwise,
without either the prior written permission of the
publishers or a licence permitting restricted copying
in the United Kingdom issued by the Copyright
Licensing Agency Ltd, 90 Tottenham Court Road,
London W1T 4LP (www.cla.co.uk).

Edited by Jenny Siklós and Paul Mason
Designed by Tim Mayer
Picture Research by Lynda Lines and Frances Bailey
Production by Duncan Gilbert
The consultant, Dr. Robert Stern, works as a part-time
analyst for the US State Department, primarily as part
of the War on Terror. He is a former Associate
Director for Counter-Terrorism.

Originated by Modern Age
Printed and bound in China by South China
Printing Company Ltd

ISBN 1 844 43203 3
10 09 08 07 06
10 9 8 7 6 5 4 3 2 1

British Library Cataloguing in Publication Data
Downing, David, 1946-
  The making of the Middle East. - (The Middle East)
  1.The Middle East - History - Juvenile literature
  I.Title
  956

Acknowledgements
The author and publisher are grateful to the
following for permission to reproduce copyright
material: AKG-Images p. **15** (Ullstein Bild); Corbis
pp. **10** (Ali Jasmin/ Reuters), **13** (Sean Sexton),
23 (Bettmann), **25** (Bettmann), **26** (Bettmann),
27 (Bettmann), **37** (Bettmann), **38** (David
Rubinger), **40** (Greg Smith), **44** (Bettmann);
Getty Images pp. **4** (David Silverman), **9** (Louai
Beshara/AFP), **14** (Hulton Archive), **19** (Percival
Richards/Hulton Archive), **20** (Hulton Archive),
21 (Keystone/Hulton Archive), **29** (James
Whitmore/Time & Life Pictures), **34** (Terry
Fincher/Hulton Archive), **35** (Central Press/Hulton
Archive), **36** (Daniel Rosenblum/Hulton Archive),
39 (Bernard Gotfryd/Hulton Archive), **41** (Hulton
Archive), **42** (Hulton Archive), **43** (David
Rubinger/Time & Life Pictures), **45** (AFP), **47**
(Spencer Platt); Panos Pictures p. **6** (Mark
Henley); Popperfoto.com p. **30**; Reuters p. **5**
(Ammar Awad); Topfoto.co.uk pp. **1**, **7**, **11**, **17**,
28, **32**, **33**.

Cover photograph shows President Gamal Abdul
Nasser of Egypt being carried through the streets
of Port Said after British and French troops were
forced to withdraw from the Suez Canal Zone in
1956 (Popperfoto.com).

Map illustrations by Encompass Graphics Ltd.

Every effort has been made to contact copyright
holders of any material reproduced in this book.
Any omissions will be rectified in subsequent
printings if notice is given to the publishers.

The paper used to print this book comes from
sustainable resources.

Contents

Some words are shown in **bold**, like this. You can find out what they mean by looking in the Glossary.

A Region in Turmoil

Turn on the TV news in the early 21st century. Natural disasters such as floods, fires, earthquakes and tidal waves seem to strike almost at random. Political disasters, on the other hand, seem much more likely in some places than others. The Middle East, in particular, has had more than its fair share of violent upheavals.

It is 2005 in Israel and Israeli-occupied Palestine. A young Arab woman steps aboard a crowded bus in an Israeli city. A few seconds later, she detonates the explosives wrapped around her waist. She and several Israeli **civilians** are killed instantly. Others are wounded, some seriously.

WHAT IS THE MIDDLE EAST?

There is no universally accepted definition of the Middle East. Some definitions stretch as far west as Morocco, and as far east as Afghanistan. Some include Turkey, Sudan and even the ex-Soviet republics of Central Asia. The core countries, however, usually include Egypt, Israel, Jordan, Syria, Lebanon, Iraq, Iran and the states of the Arabian Peninsula.

A **suicide bomber** strikes in Jerusalem in January 2004. Israeli police and rescue workers surround the ruined bus in which eleven civilians were murdered.

> **"** Everyone I spoke to heard the plane. One man, so shocked by the headless corpses he had just seen, could say only two words. 'Roar, flash', he kept saying and then closed his eyes so tight the muscles rippled behind them. **"**
>
> *(Journalist Robert Fisk reporting an attack by a US warplane on an Iraqi target during the 2003 war in Iraq)*

A few hours later, an Israeli jet bombs a Palestinian home in the **occupied territories**, killing a man they claim is a **terrorist** leader. His family die too, and the families in the rooms above and below.

It is 2005 in Iraq. American soldiers inch along a desert highway in their armoured vehicle, anxiously scanning the roadside for attackers. They believe they have come to **liberate** the country from a cruel **dictator**, to turn it into a **democracy**. Many Iraqis do not see it that way, and some are even trying to kill the soldiers.

A room somewhere in the Middle East in 2005. Members of Al-Qaeda, the terrorist group that attacked the USA on 11 September 2001, sit around a table. They are discussing their plans for the next attack. A map of a city is brought out. A Western target, because the West is their enemy.

But why do they see the West as their enemy? Why have the Israelis and the Palestinians failed to make peace? What is it about the Middle East that generates so much conflict?

Palestinian children throw rocks at an Israeli tank in the West Bank city of Ramallah during September 2002.

Ancient Times

Civilization began in the region now known as the Middle East. It was in the valleys of the Nile and the Tigris-Euphrates rivers that crops were first grown around 8000 BCE. In the hundreds of years that followed, the first cities were built, and writing was invented. Three of the world's greatest religions, Judaism, Christianity and Islam, were born in the Middle East.

The city-states of the region often fought with each other. Empires rose and fell. But until the final **millennium** BCE, there was little to fear from the world outside. Those who came to the region, either as would-be conquerors or migrants, were soon absorbed into the existing population. Middle Easterners felt that they lived in the centre of the world.

THE JEWS

The Jews were one of many Semitic peoples living in the Middle East during ancient times. In the first millennium BCE, they had their own state in much of the area now occupied by Israel. Later Jewish rebellions against the Romans led to their expulsion from the area, and their scattering throughout the rest of the known world.

Modern buildings line the ancient banks of the River Nile in the Egyptian capital, Cairo.

This picture map shows how Jerusalem may have looked in ancient times.

In the meantime, Middle Eastern traders reached out. Their new boats sailed across the Mediterranean and the Persian Gulf, bringing copper and silver from Spain. Their camels carried wool from Turkey, and gold and ivory from Africa. Their known world was getting bigger. In nearby southern Europe, new states and empires came into being.

In the 4th century BCE, a Macedonian Greek, Alexander the Great, led the first major European invasion of the Middle East. He conquered all but Arabia. Three hundred years later, it was the turn of the Romans. The wealth and fame of the region's cities made them worthwhile prizes. Its geographical position, at the crossroads of Asia, Africa and Europe, gave it **strategic** importance. For hundreds of years, the peoples of the Middle East found themselves caught between Europeans pushing east and Asians pushing west.

❝ Since Alexander secured the Nile before embarking on his oriental conquests, no empire has ventured to claim world dominion without first asserting its authority over the Middle East. ❞
(British historian John Keay)

The Arab Empire

In the 7th century CE, the relationship between Europe and the Middle East was again turned upside-down. Following the long breakup of the Roman Empire, much of Europe had slid backwards into what became known as the **Dark Ages**. At the same time, a new religion called Islam was born in the Middle East. Its early followers created an empire stretching east into Asia, and west into Africa and Europe.

Islam was founded by the Prophet Mohammed in the Arabian city of Mecca. According to Mohammed, the Islamic holy book, the **Qur'an**, was revealed to him in a series of visions. He then began preaching and gathering followers. In 622 CE he and his fellow-believers, or Muslims, were forced out of Mecca, but re-established themselves in nearby Medina. Several victories over larger Meccan forces followed, and by the time of Mohammed's death in 632 CE, most of the Arabian Peninsula was under Muslim control.

This map shows the extent to which Islam had spread by 750 CE.

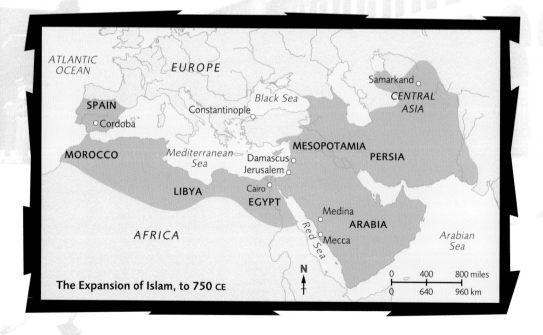

The Expansion of Islam, to 750 CE

Children playing in the courtyard of the Umayyad Mosque, Damascus.

Driven on by religious enthusiasm, Mohammed's followers sought to extend their empire. Outside Arabia, the Middle East was divided between the Byzantine and Persian Empires, both weakened by a long war with each other. Neither proved a match for the Arab armies that now attacked them. Nor, for many years, did anyone else. By the middle of the 8th century CE, the whole Middle East, North Africa, Spain and much of Central Asia had been conquered.

This Arab Empire lasted less than a century as a single unit. However, its parts, and the civilization they created, survived for around five hundred years. The artistic and scientific achievements of the Abbasid Caliphate in the Middle East, the Fatimid Caliphate in North Africa and the Umayyad Caliphate in Spain were enormous, far surpassing those of Europe in the same period.

> **" Baghdad [was turned into] the greatest centre of culture, learning and luxury in the world, at a time when the leaders of Europe could not even write their own names. "**
>
> (Historian Anthony Nutting, emphasizing the different levels of development in the Arab and European worlds of the 8th and 9th centuries CE)

THE CRUSADES

Between the 11th and 12th centuries CE, European armies took temporary control of the Holy Land. These Crusades were regarded as barbarian invasions by the Arabs, and they have never been forgotten. The Al-Qaeda terrorist leader Osama bin Laden still calls Western states who intervene in Middle East affairs 'Crusader states'.

Decline and Fall of the Arab Empire

The Arab Empire slowly lost its unity. The territory it covered was huge, and the highly populated regions were cut off from each other by wide deserts. Ambitious local leaders defied the central government, and created independent states of their own. And once independent, they fought wars against each other.

An Iraqi Muslim lashes himself with chains during the Shi'ite festival of *Ashura*.

Religious divisions played a part. As early as the late 7th century CE, a dispute over the political and religious leadership of Islam led to a crucial split. The losers in this dispute evolved their own form of Islam, and were called **Shi'ite Muslims**. They became dominant in Persia (the future Iran) and southern Iraq. The winners, who included around 90 per cent of the total, became known as **Sunni Muslims**. Outbreaks of hostility between these two branches of Islam continue to this day.

THE ARABS

The original Arabs were a Semitic people who lived in the Arabian Peninsula and spoke Arabic. During the years of conquest and empire, they mixed with the other peoples of the Middle East. Most of these other peoples converted to Islam, became Arabic-speakers and came to consider themselves as Arabs.

The Alhambra Palace in Granada, southern Spain, which was built during the years of Muslim rule in Spain.

Early in the 13th century, the long decline of the Arab world became a steep fall. In far-off Mongolia, an obscure tribal chieftain named Genghis Khan united the various Mongol tribes and turned them into a ferociously effective army. There were four great centres of Islamic culture in the Middle East at this time: the cities of Samarkand, Baghdad, Damascus and Cairo. Genghis destroyed the first, his grandson Hulagu destroyed the second and third. Only Cairo escaped. The Mongol destruction of everything from libraries to irrigation systems set the Middle East back hundreds of years.

> **❝ To be an Arab is a way of living. Arabs are deeply aware of their glorious past and of the classic status of their language. They have a passion for life and for the future. ❞**
> (Jacques Berque, scholar of Islam)

Europe, by contrast, was spared. The Mongol armies, poised to attack Western Europe, were suddenly recalled when their leader Genghis Khan's son, Ogodei, died in Mongolia. The balance between Europe and the Middle East tilted once more. While Europe moved forwards into a period of artistic and scientific achievement (the **Renaissance**), the Middle East became little more than a backwater with a glorious past.

New Intruders in the Middle East

Since the 9th century CE, waves of Turkic-speaking peoples had been moving west from their Central Asian homeland into present-day Ukraine, Iran and Turkey. In the late 14th century CE, one such group, the Ottoman Turks, controlled a small area of north-west Anatolia (modern Turkey). Three centuries later their empire stretched to include south-east Europe, North Africa and most of the Middle East.

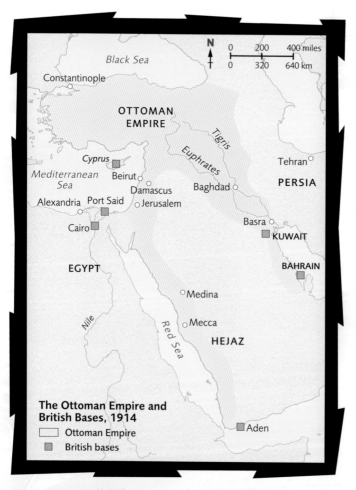

The Ottoman Empire and British Bases, 1914

☐ Ottoman Empire
■ British bases

As the Ottoman Turks were Muslims, they did nothing to change the Islamic character of the Middle East. Their leader, the reigning Sultan, became the spiritual head of Islam. Other religions were tolerated, however. The reunification of the area under one authority also brought significant benefits in trade, peace and prosperity for most of the inhabitants of the Empire.

This map shows the Middle East in 1914, including British military bases and the Ottoman Empire.

Like the rulers of the Arab and Mongol Empires, the rulers of the Ottoman Empire eventually lost effective control over their more distant provinces. By the early 19th century, for example, Egypt was basically independent. Many observers expected the empire to disintegrate before many decades had passed. Left to its own devices, it might well have done so. Instead, it was propped up by new intruders, the British and the French. Their interest in the Middle East was mainly strategic. The region lay along the land route to their **colonies** in South and South-east Asia. The Ottoman Empire, by promoting stability in the region and providing a barrier against Russian expansion southwards, helped protect that route.

Until the end of the 19th century, the Middle East itself had nothing that the British or French wanted. But this was about to change.

> **The British repeatedly claimed that they had no designs on Egypt but no one believed them for long. Once [Prime Minister] Disraeli had acquired the Suez Canal shares [in 1875], [Great] Britain's physical presence on the Nile seemed only a matter of time.**
> (Historian Jan Morris)

The northern end of the Suez Canal in the early years of the 20th century.

THE SUEZ CANAL
The Suez Canal, which cuts across Egypt to join the Mediterranean Sea with the Persian Gulf, was built by the French in the 1860s. Ownership soon passed to the British. As the canal provided the shortest route to India (and, in later years, the Persian Gulf oilfields), its safety was vital to the British. They decided that they needed a permanent military presence in Egypt to guard it.

The Importance of Oil

There were two reasons why the Middle East became one of the world's most important regions in the 20th century. One was the rapidly growing importance of oil in the world's richer countries. The other was the discovery of huge reserves of oil in the Middle East.

Early oil prospectors at work at Petroleum Springs, Dalaki, in Persia (what is now Iran) in about 1890.

Until the final decades of the 19th century, oil had mostly been used for lighting and lubrication. In the 20th century, it became the main source of energy for industry in general and transport in particular. Oil was cheaper to get out of the ground than coal, and cheaper to move around. Even before World War I (1914–1918), the British Royal Navy was converting its ships to burn oil rather than coal. And the use of road transport was dramatically increasing, particularly in the USA.

❝ It is a gospel fact ... that a fleet with oil fuel will have an overwhelming advantage over a coal fleet. ❞
(Admiral Sir John Fisher of the British navy, writing in 1902)

MAKING SURE OF OIL

After World War I, the British wanted their own source of oil. When they set up the new Arab state of Iraq in the Tigris-Euphrates valley, they made sure it included the oil-rich Mosul region within its borders. The fact that this region was mostly inhabited by Kurds, rather than Arabs, was not considered important at the time, but would lead to problems in the future.

A new oil pipeline from Iraq to the Mediterranean reaches the Palestinian coast in 1930.

The first major oil discoveries in the Middle East were made by the British, in southern Iran. Production began in 1908. Between World Wars I and II, more large discoveries were made in other areas. These were in northern Iraq, around the head of the Persian Gulf, and, eventually, in the Arabian desert. The Middle East, it would later turn out, had around two-thirds of the world's supply of oil buried beneath its sands and offshore waters.

This potential wealth would eventually offer the lucky countries a chance to fund a better life for at least some of their people. But it would also provoke more and more interference from those countries beyond the Middle East who depended on its oil to run their economies. As far as these countries were concerned, the region was now too important to leave alone.

World War I

World War I brought about a change of control in the Middle East. The Ottoman Empire fought on the losing side, and by 1918, its troops had been expelled from the region. The Ottomans were replaced by the British and the French, except in central Arabia, which was left to the Arabs.

In 1916 the British and French agreed to divide the Middle East between them. They kept this so-called 'Sykes-Picot Agreement' secret because they needed help from the Arabs and the Jews, both of whom opposed such a division. They needed Arab military help against the Turks. And they hoped that the support of influential Jewish communities in Russia and the USA would keep Russia fighting and bring the USA into the war.

This map shows how the British and the French planned to divide the Middle East between them under the terms of the Sykes-Picot Agreement of 1916. However this was not how the region was ruled in the years after World War I (see page 18).

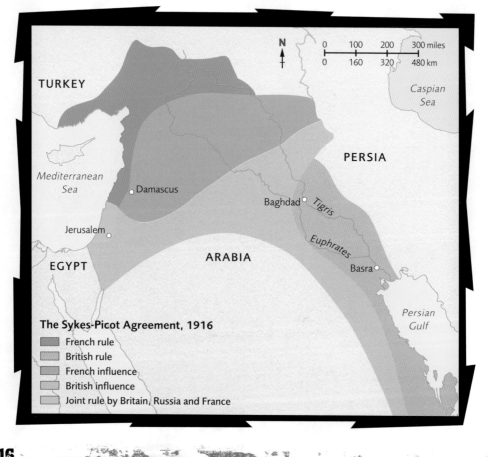

0 100 200 300 miles
0 160 320 480 km

TURKEY

Caspian Sea

PERSIA

Mediterranean Sea

Damascus

Baghdad

Tigris

Jerusalem

Euphrates

ARABIA

EGYPT

Basra

Persian Gulf

The Sykes-Picot Agreement, 1916

- French rule
- British rule
- French influence
- British influence
- Joint rule by Britain, Russia and France

In a series of letters between Sir Henry McMahon (the British High Commissioner in Egypt) and Hussein ibn Ali (leader of Arabia's most powerful tribe), the British effectively promised the Arabs independence in return for their military support. The Arabs kept their side of the bargain, but the British did not. A few Arab leaders would be given important positions after the war, but the ordinary people of the Middle East simply exchanged Turkish rule for British or French rule. Many Arabs felt betrayed.

> **" Luckily, we have been very careful indeed to commit ourselves to nothing whatsoever. "**
> (Gilbert Clayton, head of British Intelligence in Cairo during World War I, stating what he believed Britain had promised the Arabs)

Since the late 19th century, the **Zionist** movement had been campaigning for a new Jewish homeland, preferably in Ottoman Palestine. In 1917 the British Foreign Minister Arthur Balfour wrote to the prominent Jewish banker Lord Rothschild, promising British support for this. At the same time, he promised to safeguard the rights of non-Jews in Palestine. Keeping both promises was virtually impossible, and the British ended up keeping neither.

LAWRENCE OF ARABIA

The British officer who helped persuade the Arabs to join Great Britain's war against the Ottoman Empire was Colonel T. E. Lawrence. He fought alongside them and wrote a famous book, *Seven Pillars of Wisdom*, about his experiences. When the British government broke its promises to the Arabs, Lawrence also felt betrayed.

T. E. Lawrence (at the wheel) with some of Britain's Arab allies during World War I.

New Arrangements for the Middle East

The new arrangements for the Middle East were agreed at the post-war **Versailles peace talks** in early 1919. These arrangements were, essentially, an updating of the secret agreement that Great Britain and France had come to in 1916 (see page 16). Since Arabia's enormous oilfields had not yet been discovered, that region was left to take care of itself. The rest of the Middle East was divided between the British and French.

> **❝** 'I say, Lawrence,' Churchill offered, looking rather worried, 'are these people dangerous? They don't seem too pleased to see us.' **❞**
>
> *(Winston Churchill, the future British prime minister, talking to T. E. Lawrence ('Lawrence of Arabia'). During a tour of Palestine in 1921, they had run into an Arab demonstration against Zionism.)*

A series of new states were created: Lebanon and Syria in the French area and Iraq, Palestine and Transjordan in the British area. The **League of Nations**, a new organization set up to help regulate international affairs, then gave the British and French '**mandates**' (the right) to rule these states.

This map shows the Middle East mandates created by the League of Nations in 1922.

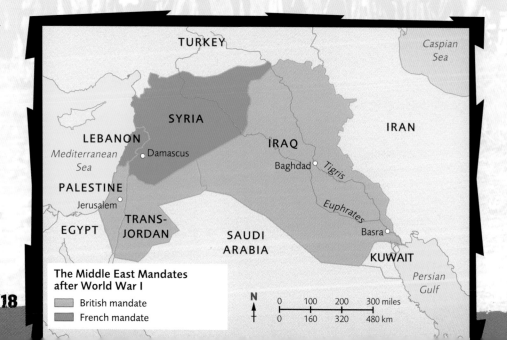

TURKEY

Caspian Sea

SYRIA

IRAN

LEBANON

Mediterranean Sea

Damascus

IRAQ

Baghdad

Tigris

PALESTINE

Jerusalem

Euphrates

TRANS-JORDAN

EGYPT

SAUDI ARABIA

Basra

KUWAIT

Persian Gulf

The Middle East Mandates after World War I

☐ British mandate
☐ French mandate

N

0	100	200	300 miles
0	160	320	480 km

The borders of these new states were drawn up with little thought for the future needs of the people within these countries. The Mediterranean coastal region of the French area, for example, was home to many Christian Arabs, and the new Lebanon was almost equally divided between Christians and Muslims. Transjordan was split between nomadic (roaming) and settled Arabs, and Iraq between Sunni Arabs, Shi'ite Muslims and Kurds. The Kurdish people found themselves occupying corners of four different countries: Turkey, Iraq, Iran and Syria. When the French and British eventually left the region, their bad decisions caused decades of problems for the local populations to deal with.

TURKEY

The heartland of the Ottoman Empire, comprising Anatolia and a small corner of Europe, became modern Turkey (see map on page 12). In general this state has looked west towards Europe. It has only intervened in Middle Eastern affairs when Kurdish rebellions in Iraq or Iran have threatened to stir up the Kurdish minority in Turkey.

For the moment, however, the only big change was in the colour of the flag flying above the local military post. Foreign soldiers still patrolled the streets and chose the local rulers. Serious prospecting for oil had only just begun. The British and French were supposed to be preparing the mandated territories for independence and democracy, but seemed in no hurry to do so. The people of the Middle East were beginning to wonder just how independent, and just how democratic, their new countries would turn out to be.

This photo shows Kurds who fought against the Ottoman Empire. Though they were promised independence by the Allies in 1920, the Kurds were soon crushed by the new Turkey.

Between the Wars

Political and economic progress in the Middle East between the wars was extremely limited. None of the mandate territories received genuine independence, and none were encouraged to introduce any real democracy. The British failed to find any permanent solution to the particular problem of Palestine, which was a problem they had themselves largely created.

INDEPENDENCE?

In 1925 the Egyptian King tried to change Egyptian election law. In 1926 the election winners tried to offer an anti-British candidate for prime minister. In 1927 the Egyptian government tried to end British control of the Egyptian Army. On each occasion a British warship steamed into Alexandria harbour, to remind everyone who was in charge.

Wherever they happened to be, the European powers made sure of retaining ultimate control. For example, both Egypt (in 1922) and Iraq (in 1932) were officially granted independence. But British troops remained in both countries and real power remained in their hands. The local elite, including landowners, merchants and religious leaders, were taught that their interests lay in siding with the Europeans, and not with their own people. As things were, the Europeans claimed, real democracy would be far too dangerous. The stability of their countries would be put at risk, not to mention their wealth and their lives.

General Allenby, the British High Commissioner in Egypt from 1919 to 1925, is given a ceremonial send-off as he prepares to leave Egypt.

In Palestine, the British were trapped by the expectations and fears they had raised with their promises. In the years between the world wars, they allowed enough Jewish **immigration** to anger the Arabs, but not enough to please the Jews. Violent confrontations between the two peoples became more frequent during the 1930s.

> ❝ When I was a little child, every time I saw aeroplanes flying overhead I used to shout: 'Oh God Almighty, may a calamity overtake the English.' ❞
> *(Gamal Abdul Nasser, the future president of Egypt)*

A Jewish house in Tel Aviv is set on fire during the Arab uprising of 1936.

In Arabia another outside power had arrived in the Middle East. A series of tribal wars in the 1920s ended with the victory of the Saudi tribe, and the proclamation of a unified Kingdom of Saudi Arabia in 1932. The following year the new Saudi Royal Family found itself in need of money, and sold an **oil concession** to the American Standard Oil company. This was the beginning of a Saudi-American relationship that would prove vital to both sides.

World War II and After

In World War II, the only large-scale fighting in the Middle East was in Egypt's Western Desert. There were, however, significant displays of popular support for the German cause in Syria, Iraq, Egypt and Iran. It was not that these peoples loved the Germans. It was more that they hated the British and French.

THE SHAHS OF IRAN

The British helped Reza Khan seize power in Iran in 1921. As Shah (king) from 1925, he offered stability, both for the country and for British oil interests. In 1941, alarmed by his pro-German leanings, the British forced him out. His son Mohammed Reza Pahlavi became the new Shah, a position he held until Iran's Islamic Revolution in 1979.

When the war ended, the British, French and Americans had important decisions to make. As oil continued to grow in importance, so did the Middle East. Stability was essential, but harder and harder to guarantee. Throughout the non-European world, there were demands for an end to European rule. In Palestine events seemed to be lurching out of control. What could the Western powers do to keep the area quiet?

The French had already decided against staying in Syria and Lebanon. Neither had any oil, and both were granted independence. The British granted independence to Transjordan, which also had no oil. They then tried to make the continuing British military presence in Egypt and Iraq less obvious. In Egypt, for example, they shifted their troops into the **Suez Canal Zone** in 1947, and withdrew them altogether in 1954. In the Persian Gulf area, however, they continued to control Kuwait and the other small kingdoms of the Persian Gulf (the future Qatar, Bahrain and United Arab Emirates). The USA decided to strengthen its relationship with Saudi Arabia, and in 1945 President Roosevelt met King Ibn Saud for talks on a US warship.

> **" Arab unity is the way to Jerusalem. "**
> (A slogan from the first meeting of the Arab League in 1945. Only if the various Arab states were united, the slogan suggested, could they hope to keep Palestine.)

In Palestine the British were still trying to persuade the local Arabs and Jews to share the country. Neither was prepared to do so. Attacks on each other and the British grew more frequent.

US President Franklin D. Roosevelt (seated on right) talking with the Saudi Arabian king, Ibn Saud, on an American warship moored in Egypt's Great Bitter Lake, in February 1945.

The Birth of Israel

❝ I am certain that the world will judge the Jewish state by what it shall do with the Arabs. ❞
(Chaim Weizmann, early Zionist leader and first president of Israel)

In 1947 the British decided that their mandate in Palestine had become too costly, in both money and human lives. They handed the problem over to the **United Nations**, which voted on 29 November 1947 to **partition** (divide) Palestine between Jews and Arabs.

International sympathy for the terrible sufferings of the Jewish people in World War II played a large part in this decision. It also affected the way it was carried out. Jews, who formed 33 per cent of the population, were given a generous 50 per cent of the land. Not surprisingly, the Palestinian Arabs rejected the UN partition plan. Over the next six months, the territory descended into **civil war**. On 14 May 1948, the mandate officially ended. That same evening the new state of Israel was proclaimed by Jewish leaders in Jerusalem.

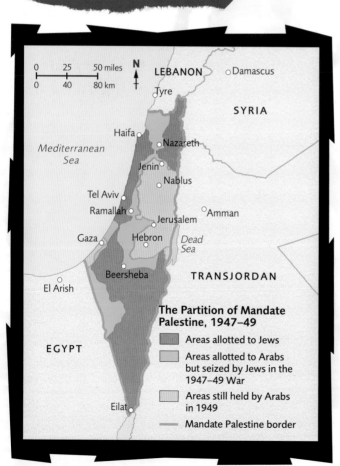

The Partition of Mandate Palestine, 1947–49

- Areas allotted to Jews
- Areas allotted to Arabs but seized by Jews in the 1947–49 War
- Areas still held by Arabs in 1949
- Mandate Palestine border

This map shows how the United Nations partitioned Mandate Palestine between Jews and Arabs in 1947. The green shading shows Arab areas that were seized by Israel during the war of 1947–1949.

The next day, the armies of five neighbouring states, Egypt, Transjordan, Syria, Iraq and Lebanon, crossed the border in support of their fellow Arabs. These armies, badly equipped and badly led, were soon defeated. When the war ended in early 1949, the borders of the new Israel had expanded to include 70 per cent of the original mandate territory. About 750,000 Palestinian Arabs had become **refugees**.

Arabs load their belongings onto a truck, after Jewish fighters occupied their village during the civil war in Palestine in 1947–1949.

For the Jews of Palestine and elsewhere, this was cause for celebration. For the Arabs of Palestine and elsewhere, it was a disaster. The Palestinian Arabs believed their land had been stolen, and half a century later they would still be trying to get it back. For Arabs elsewhere, the defeat was a terrible humiliation. They blamed their own governments, who were at least partly responsible. Most of all, they blamed the Western powers for giving them such governments, and for supporting the creation of Israel.

THE WEST BANK AND GAZA

The Arabs held on to 30 per cent of Palestine. The Gaza Strip was taken over by Egypt, and the West Bank was taken over by Jordan (previously Transjordan). Both areas were then occupied by Israel in 1967. Egypt and Jordan eventually renounced any claim to them, arguing that they should form the basis of a new Palestinian state.

Arab Nationalism

The British and French might have surrendered the driver's seat in the Middle East, but they still owned the vehicle, and they were still giving orders from the back seat. Many Arabs, particularly the young and the educated, simply wanted them gone. For many years these Arabs had wanted to rule themselves, and to **modernize** their societies. They called themselves **Arab nationalists**.

> **"** The basic principles of the Ba'ath Party were unity and freedom inside an Arab nation. The party also based itself on the belief that Arabs had a special mission to end Western colonialism. **"**
>
> (Encyclopaedia of the Orient)

During the 1950s, Arab nationalists came to power in Egypt, Syria and Iraq. In Syria a number of military governments succeeded each other, some more nationalist than others. In both Egypt (1952) and Iraq (1958), nationalist army officers seized power from kings and political elites supported by the British.

Most Arab nationalists were either **Ba'athists** or Nasserites. The Ba'ath Party, which had been founded in Syria by Michael Aflaq in the 1940s, was strongest in Syria and Iraq. Nasserites, named after the new Egyptian leader Gamal Abdul Nasser, could be found throughout the Arab Middle East. The two groups did not agree on everything. However, they did agree on essentials, including being anti-Western, anti-Israel, pro-modernization and pro-Arab unity.

The possessions of the murdered Iraqi royal family are spread out in front of their former palace in the aftermath of the revolution of 1958.

Iranian Prime Minister Mohammed Mossadegh addresses a crowd in Tehran during his oil dispute with the West, September 1951.

MOSSADEGH'S FALL

It was not only the Arab countries in the Middle East that saw a surge of anti-Western feeling. In the early 1950s, anti-Western nationalists in Iran, under the leadership of Mohammed Mossadegh, tried to seize control of the country's oil industry. The pro-Western Shah, Mohammed Reza Pahlavi, was temporarily forced to leave the country. In 1953, however, Mossadegh was overthrown by Western intelligence agents. The Shah was then allowed to return.

In other Arab countries, the Arab nationalists were kept from power. These countries, which included the major oil producers, were still ruled by unelected kings and their families. They saw Arab nationalism as a threat to their wealth and power. In public, they were happy to shout nationalist slogans, as insulting Israel cost them nothing. In private, they made a bargain with the West. They would ensure stability and the flow of oil if the West agreed not to criticize their lack of democracy. The Arab kings also wanted the West to promise, as a last resort, to save them from their own people.

The Cold War

At the end of World War II, the **free enterprise** USA and the **communist** Soviet Union emerged as the two main world powers. The two states organized their societies completely differently. The USA was based on private property, and the Soviet Union had an economy run entirely by the state. There was little room for agreement between the two countries. Between 1947 and 1948, a series of disputes in Eastern Europe and Asia turned into the **Cold War**.

Nuclear weapons made a real war impossible, so the two superpowers competed with each other in every other possible way, all over the world. When one of them supplied a foreign government with financial and military aid, the other would do the same for that government's opponents. The Middle East was important for both superpowers. Oil was crucial for the USA and its Western allies. The region lay on the Soviet Union's southern doorstep.

❝ The existing vacuum in the Middle East must be filled by the United States before it is filled by Russia. ❞
(President Dwight D. Eisenhower, speaking in 1957, after British and French influence in the Middle East had virtually ended)

US President Eisenhower (left) and Mohammed Reza Pahlavi, the Shah of Iran, hold talks in Tehran in December 1959.

Soviet-made Egyptian tanks rumble through Cairo in July 1957.

THE WRONG AID

The Cold War brought some benefits to the Middle East. The superpowers did provide a certain amount of economic aid for development. This was overshadowed, however, by the huge flow of military aid. By the 1970s most Middle Eastern countries had modern armed forces, but few had modern economies.

There were communist parties in most Middle Eastern countries, but none of them were close to gaining power. The Soviets mostly ignored them, and gave their support to the Arab nationalists, whom they hoped would weaken Western influence. They gave large amounts of economic and military aid, first to Egypt, and then later to Syria and Iraq.

The USA backed the Arab **conservatives**, like their ally Saudi Arabia. They opposed the Arab nationalists, whom they feared would cause too much trouble in the region. Since Israel was also threatened by the Arab nationalists, the link between the USA and Israel grew stronger. In the Middle East, the USA came to be seen as an enemy of Arab progress and a friend of Israel.

The Suez Crisis and the Sinai War

The major developments in the post-war Middle East were the birth of Israel, the growth of Arab nationalism and the intrusion of the Cold War. These all became knotted together into one crisis during the summer and autumn of 1956.

As part of his plans to modernize Egypt, Nasser proposed a huge dam on the River Nile at Aswan. When the Soviet Union hinted that it might fund this project, the USA reacted by making an offer of its own. But the Americans then decided that Nasser was too much of an extremist, and withdrew the offer. Nasser decided that there was only one way he could pay for the dam. He would **nationalize** the Suez Canal, and use the toll money that had previously gone to its British and French owners. In June 1956 his troops took control of the Canal Zone.

The UK and France decided to take it back from Nasser, but needed a good excuse to do so. Nasser was offering reasonable compensation to the British and French, and had done nothing illegal. The USA advised the UK and France not to take military action. Instead of following this advice, they made a deal with Israel. At a secret meeting in October, the three states agreed that Israeli forces would advance across the Egyptian Sinai Peninsula towards the Canal. The UK and France would then invade the Canal Zone, claiming that they had only come to keep the Egyptians and Israelis apart.

> **❝ What's all this nonsense about isolating Nasser or 'neutralizing' him? I want him destroyed, can't you understand? ❞**
> (British Prime Minister Anthony Eden, shouting at one of his civil servants during the Suez Crisis of 1956)

The plan was carried out in November. No one believed the British and French, and within weeks they were pressured into accepting United Nations troops in place of their own. The Israelis, who had easily beaten the Egyptians in Sinai, were also pressured into withdrawing. Nasser had lost the military battles, but he had won the war. Egyptian ownership of the Canal was confirmed.

President Nasser is carried through the streets of Port Said by jubilant Egyptians after the British withdrawal from the Suez Canal Zone in 1956.

WHY DID ISRAEL JOIN THE UK AND FRANCE?

Israel joined the attack on Egypt for a number of reasons. They wanted to stop the cross-border guerrilla raids that were coming from Egypt. Israel also feared that a successful Nasser would unite the other Arab states against it. And like the British and French, they hoped to humiliate and destroy Nasser.

Ten Years of Arab Optimism

The Suez Crisis was a disaster for the UK and France, who lost most of their remaining influence in the Middle East. It was better news for the USA, whose refusal to support the UK and France briefly boosted their popularity with the Arabs. The main winners, though, were Nasser and Arab nationalism.

Egypt's President Nasser with Salah El Bitar (left) and Michael Aflaq (right), the two founders of the Syrian Ba'ath Party, in March 1963.

For the next few years, it seemed as if Nasser could do little wrong. The Aswan Dam, finally built with Soviet help, provided electricity to expand the Egyptian economy. A proposed union with Syria looked set to extend Egypt's influence, and encourage a wider Arab unity. As the 1960s unfolded, many Arabs started to believe that the bad times were over. Economic development was underway. Arab status in the world was finally rising. Even the eventual failure of the union between Egypt and Syria couldn't take away the feeling of optimism.

REVOLUTION IN IRAQ

In 1958 Arab nationalists seized power in Iraq. Both Nasserites and Ba'athists were involved, but the Nasserites came out on top. In 1968 the Nasserites were overthrown by the Ba'athists. Ahmad Hassan al-Bakr became the new president. However, it soon became clear that the man with the real power was his young deputy, Saddam Hussein.

> **❝ A mere hour after Radio Baghdad had announced the end of the monarchy, well over a million people were celebrating in the streets... ❞**
>
> *(Arab author Said K. Aburish describing the popular enthusiasm for the 1958 revolution in Iraq)*

The success of the nationalists made the conservative Arab regimes in Jordan and the Persian Gulf nervous. They fought back by taking their own Arab nationalist actions. They gave financial aid to poorer Arab states and the Palestinian refugees. At the same time, the apparent weakness of the West encouraged the Arab oil-producers to demand a higher share of the Western oil companies' profits. OPEC (the Organization of Petroleum Exporting Countries) was founded in 1960 to present a united front against the rich oil-importing countries.

The Arabs seemed to be growing stronger. However, Israel was the one glaring reminder of their weakness. By 1967 Nasser, in particular, had decided that a reckoning was both necessary and possible. Few historians believe that Nasser wanted an actual war. However, a war was exactly what his aggressive words and action led to.

An OPEC conference takes place in Kuwait in December 1966.

The war of 1967, also known as the Six Day War and the June War, was a defining moment in Arab-Israeli relations. Its consequences are still with us today. The Arabs provoked this war in a number of ways. They moved their troops to border areas, they refused to allow Israeli shipping in their waters and they made loud threats. However, it was the Israelis who actually set the war in motion, though they claimed they acted for defensive reasons.

Disaster came to the Arabs out of a clear blue sky. On the morning of 5 June 1967, the Israeli Air Force launched surprise attacks on airbases in Egypt, Syria, Jordan and Iraq. The Arab planes were destroyed on the ground. Lacking air cover, their armies proved no match for the smaller, more efficient Israeli army. In six days the Israelis took Sinai and the Gaza Strip from Egypt, the Golan Heights from Syria and all of Jordan west of the River Jordan, including East Jerusalem. The Israelis were in no hurry to hand any of it back. The occupation had begun.

These burnt-out Egyptian aircraft at El Arish base in Sinai were destroyed during the Israeli air strikes that opened the Arab-Israeli War of 1967.

These Egyptian prisoners were captured by Israeli forces in Sinai in June 1967.

❝ Nobody had been prepared for defeat on such a shattering scale... The Israelis were jubilant, the Arab world was in a state of total confusion. ❞
(Arab journalist Mohammed Heikal)

❝ Out of the ashes of this disastrous war will arise a phoenix of a free Arab Palestine. ❞
(Former Palestinian leader Yasser Arafat)

Arab nationalist hopes were in tatters. As in 1948 and 1949, there was anger and confusion at the completeness of the Arab failure. The USA was blamed for supporting Israel, particularly after the war. This was mostly due to the US **veto** of a United Nations resolution demanding that the occupied territories be returned without condition.

For the Palestinian Arabs, this was a turning point. They now doubted that the Arab states would ever win back their land for them. The Palestinians realized that they would have to do it for themselves. Over the next six years, various sections of the **PLO** (Palestine Liberation Organization) tried to fight their own war against Israel. But neither guerrilla war nor terrorism brought them any success.

THE PLO
The Palestinian Liberation Organization was founded in 1964 as a loose alliance of smaller groups. The largest, Fatah, was led by Yasser Arafat for more than 40 years. The group responsible for most of the major terrorist outrages of the early 1970s was the PFLP (the Popular Front for the Liberation of Palestine).

The War of 1973

In November 1967 the United Nations **Security Council** passed Resolution 242. This called for Israel to withdraw from the territories it had just occupied. It also called for the Arabs to recognize Israel's right to exist. Both refused.

Over the next few years, the USA tried, without success, to get the two sides talking to each other. Between 1969 and 1970, Egypt tried to wear down Israeli resistance by bombarding their positions along the Suez Canal. However, the Israelis hit back twice as hard, bombing targets deep inside Egypt. After Nasser died in 1970, his successor, President Anwar Sadat, decided that only another war could break the stalemate. Syria, under its new President Hafez al-Assad, was willing to join him.

The war of 1973, also known as the October War, Ramadan War and Yom Kippur War, began on 6 October. This time the Arabs took the Israelis by surprise. As Egyptian troops stormed across the Suez Canal, Syrian troops poured into the Golan Heights. For a few days, it looked as though Sadat and Assad's gamble had succeeded. But in the end, the Arab forces were still no match for the Israelis. Within a week the tide had turned, and Israeli tanks were pushing into Egypt and Syria.

Israeli tanks climbing the road to Syria in October 1973.

Mile-long lines for petrol form in Englewood, New Jersey, USA, during the global oil shortages that followed the Arab-Israeli War of 1973.

Others intervened. On 17 October an OPEC meeting in Kuwait announced that oil production would be cut back until Israel withdrew from the occupied territories. A day later, angered by American arms deliveries to Israel, Saudi Arabia stopped all oil deliveries to the USA. The USA told Israel to cease operations, claiming that the Soviets would intervene if the USA did not. The Israelis did so, but only after advancing further into Egypt.

> **❝** We have fought and we shall go on fighting to liberate our land which was seized by Israeli occupation in 1967, and to find the means towards the restoration and respect of the legitimate rights of the Palestinian people. **❞**
>
> *(President Sadat of Egypt, 16 October 1973)*

A NUCLEAR ALERT

When the Israelis continued to advance into Egypt, the Soviets accused the USA of betrayal, and threatened to get involved. The USA put their nuclear forces on full alert, and the Soviets backed down. The world was given a stark reminder of just how dangerous the Middle East situation had become.

After the Wars

The Arabs had finally won some battles, yet still lost the war. This third failure would be the last. After three major wars in 25 years, the Arab states were forced to acknowledge that Israel was there to stay.

An Israeli flag flies over an Israeli settlement in the occupied West Bank. The settling of territories occupied by force is illegal under international law.

In the meantime, the Israeli occupation of Arab territory, the Gaza Strip and the West Bank, looked set to become permanent. Many Israelis refused to accept a Palestinian state in that territory, claiming that it would be a permanent threat to their security. Some wanted to cover the territory with Jewish **settlements**, and then attach it to Israel. Faced with this threat, the Palestinians eventually came to accept Israel's right to exist in return for their own state within the territories occupied since 1967. But by then the Israelis wanted more, and demanded a change in the borders, rights for their settlers and the whole of the city of Jerusalem.

JERUSALEM
The ownership of Jerusalem, with its Jewish, Christian and Muslim holy sites, has been important for many centuries. In 1949 it was divided between Israel and Jordan, but in 1967, Israel took the whole city. The Palestinians insist on East Jerusalem as their future capital, but Israel has refused to redivide the city.

Meanwhile the rest of the Arab world was coming to terms with the failure of the nationalist dream. The inability to defeat Israel was a part of this failure. However, many people in the Middle East were more worried about the lack of economic progress and effective government. Even in the oil-rich countries, the benefits of modernization had mostly gone to those at the top. This was most true in Iran, which had little to do with the Arab-Israeli dispute, and which would soon erupt in revolution.

The flow of oil to the West resumed, but at a higher price. And the richer nations had been given a dramatic reminder of how important the Middle East was to their economies. If threatened again, the West would be ready to intervene.

> **Today I have come bearing an olive branch [a traditional symbol of peace] and a freedom fighter's gun. Do not let the olive branch fall from my hand!**
>
> *(Former Palestinian leader Yasser Arafat addressing the United Nations on 13 November 1974)*

PLO leader Yasser Arafat, during his famous 'olive branch' address to the United Nations General Assembly. If the international community did not help the Palestinians, he implied, then the war with Israel would be endless.

Peace and Further Conflict

Faced with failure, the Arab states reacted in different ways. Whatever unity had existed previously soon disappeared. In 1977 Egypt's President Sadat signed a separate peace with Israel. In exchange for the return of Sinai, he recognized Israel's right to exist. However this led to him being seen as a traitor by many Arabs and Arab governments.

> ❝ Israel will be amazed to hear me say that I am prepared to go to their home, to the Knesset [the Israeli parliament] itself, and discuss things with them. ❞
> *(President Sadat of Egypt, setting in motion events that would lead to peace between his country and Israel)*

CIVIL WAR IN LEBANON (1975–1991)

The Lebanese civil war had two historical sources. One was the economic and political dominance of the minority Christian community, a dominance that the country had inherited from the French. The other was the Israeli-Palestinian conflict. When large numbers of Palestinian refugees arrived in Lebanon, they sided with the local Muslims against the Christians.

A young soldier stands guard over the ruins of the capital Beirut in 1984, during the civil war in Lebanon.

The Arabs blamed their politicians, the West and each other. As the sense of unity faded, divisions appeared. These divisions were between **left-wing** and **right-wing** political groups, Christian and Muslim, Shi'ite and Sunni, and states who rejected peace with Israel and states who did not. By the end of the 1970s, Lebanon had descended into civil war and Iran into revolution. The Kurds of Iraq were already in revolt, and the Kurds of Iran soon would be. In the 1980s a major war between Sunni-led Iraq and Shi'ite-led Iran claimed many more lives than all the Arab-Israeli wars put together.

Arab nationalism, however, was not completely dead. Saddam Hussein, the effective leader of Iraq since the early 1970s, was an Arab nationalist. Like Nasser before him, he annoyed the West by taking over their businesses in Iraq and making threats against Israel. But Saddam too would eventually fail. Saddam's war with Iran, his invasion of Kuwait, and his long conflict with the West would eventually ruin him.

Iraqi President Saddam Hussein addresses soldiers of his army in 1980, shortly before launching the war against Iran.

Long before Saddam's eventual defeat, there was a growing feeling in the Middle East that the **secular** nationalism pioneered by Nasser and the Ba'athists had failed. But what was the alternative? For many Arabs and Iranians, it could only be religion. They would reject the secular values of the West, and turn back to the traditional values of Islam.

The Turn to Islam

The idea of separating church and state, the religious and the secular, has been generally accepted in Europe and North America for over 200 years. Arab and Iranian nationalists also accepted it. Although leaders like Nasser, Mohammed Reza Shah Pahlavi of Iran and Saddam Hussein of Iraq were all Muslims, their governments were secular.

When Arab and Iranian nationalism failed to bring economic, political or military success, many people began to wonder if this type of government was right for the Middle East. From the 1970s on, there was a dramatic growth of political groups demanding Islamic government. The members of these groups were often called **Islamic fundamentalists**, because they wanted a return to what they said were the fundamentals of Islam.

There was a long tradition of such groups in the Middle East. The Muslim Brotherhood in Egypt, for example, had been banned by Nasser in the 1950s. But these groups only really gathered strength when it seemed like secular government had failed. The Iranian Revolution of 1979 was one key event. During the Revolution, the American-backed, secular Shah was replaced by the religious leader Ayatollah Khomeini. The civil war in Afghanistan (1978–1992), in which a Soviet-backed secular government was defeated by Islamic fundamentalists, was another.

Iranian demonstrators carrying portraits of Ayatollah Khomeini through the streets of Tehran on New Year's Day, 1979. Two weeks later the Shah was overthrown.

Supporters of Hamas, one of the two major Palestinian fundamentalist groups, at a rally in the West Bank town of Jericho in May 1994.

Many Islamic fundamentalists are hostile to the West. They blame Western policies and power for the poverty of many Muslim countries. They blame Western values for the corruption of Middle Eastern politics and lifestyles. In particular, they oppose the Western presence in the Middle East. Osama bin Laden, the leader of the terrorist group Al-Qaeda, has repeatedly said that the group's main aim is to drive the USA out of Saudi Arabia and the Persian Gulf.

> **My brothers, you are the new light that will destroy the darkness of materialism [an obsession with owning things]. You are the voices that echo the message of Prophet Mohammed.**
>
> (Hassan el-Banna, the founder of the Egyptian Muslim Brotherhood)

THE SPREAD OF ISLAMIC FUNDAMENTALISM

In the 1980s and 1990s, Islamic fundamentalism became an important factor in the politics of most Arab countries and movements. In Egypt, fundamentalists assassinated President Sadat and targeted Western tourists. Amongst Palestinians, new fundamentalist organizations like **Hamas** and **Islamic Jihad** gained popularity at the expense of older groups.

The Terrorist Threat

The recent military history of Arab states and movements has been a history of defeat. Israeli military strength has proved too much for both the Arab states and the Palestinian groups. American military strength has proved too much for either Arab nationalists or Islamic fundamentalists. Some Arabs and Iranians have turned to terrorism because everything else has failed.

In the 1950s the Palestinians tried cross-border raids into Israel. In 1968 they tried sending armed groups into the occupied territories. But the Israeli defenses were too good, and both tactics failed. Some Palestinian groups then tried **hijacking** planes. This tactic brought publicity to their cause, but lost them many friends. Other terrorist actions, such as the murder of Israeli athletes at the 1972 Olympics, were almost universally condemned.

Hooded (above) and masked (below) Palestinian terrorists in Munich, Germany, during the 1972 summer Olympics. Despite attempts at negotiation, the terrorists murdered eleven members of the Israeli Olympic team.

> **❝ I swear to Allah [God] that those living in America will not live in security and safety until we live in peace and security in our lands and in Palestine, and the army of infidels [non-Muslims] has departed from the land of Mohammed [Saudi Arabia]... ❞**
> *(Osama bin Laden, October 2001)*

خـاص
بالجـزيرة

Osama bin Laden, the hunted leader of Al-Qaeda. The picture is taken from a video recorded at a secret location in Afghanistan in 2001.

After the 1973 war, the main Palestinian groups gave up terrorism in favour of **diplomacy**. From the late 1980s on, these groups combined this with low-level civil war, for example, the stone-throwings of the **intifada**. When these tactics failed to produce a breakthrough, some Islamic fundamentalist Palestinian groups went back to terrorism, using suicide bombers to attack Israeli civilians.

After what they see as 50 years of US military interventions, political interference and economic control in the Middle East, the Islamic fundamentalists want the USA out. But they cannot fight them in the open, or they would be crushed. Terrorism, to a few Arabs, seems like the only way they have of fighting back. In most parts of the world the terrorist attacks of 11 September 2001 were seen as a murderous outrage. It is important to realize that some people in the Middle East saw them, no matter how mistakenly, as a blow against their oppressors.

THE BEGINNINGS OF AL-QAEDA

Between 1987 and 1988, Osama bin Laden and Abdullah Azzam created a new Muslim fundamentalist fighting organization called Al-Qaeda. Its first members were Islamic veterans of the Afghan civil war. They would fight wherever they were needed. Azzam disagreed with terrorism, but he was killed in 1989, most probably by friends of Osama bin Laden.

The three principal conflicts afflicting the Middle East in the opening decade of the 21st century have been the continuing struggle between Israel and the Palestinians, the war in Iraq and the '**War on Terror**'. The last two conflicts are relatively recent, but all three have their roots in the past.

Palestine has been a problem since the British promised it to both the Arabs and the Jews. The only acceptable solutions to the problem, two peoples sharing one state or two states side by side, were suggested by the British as early as the 1930s. But there was not enough trust for either solution to work. After 70 years of mutual violence, there is even less trust now.

This map shows the oilfields of the Middle East and the conflicts that have flared up in the region since 1948.

Reem Saleh Raiyshi, a mother of two children from the occupied Gaza Strip. Shortly after this photograph was taken she blew herself up at a border crossing point, killing at least four Israelis.

The war in Iraq, and the violent resistance to the occupation that followed it, offer numerous examples of the grip of the past. The Western powers built up Saddam in the 1980s because they thought he would help them restrain revolutionary Iran. The same Western powers' determination to keep the oil flowing was one factor in their decision to attack and overthrow Saddam. One consequence of the war was to upset relations between the Shi'ites, Sunnis and Kurds, who the British had lumped together into one country in 1918. The hostility between Sunnis and Shi'ites, of course, goes back to the 7th century CE.

The 'War on Terror' is not confined to the Middle East. However, the leaders of Al-Qaeda, the most important terrorist group, are all from there. They deeply resent the West and any Middle Eastern governments it supports. They are angry at the failure of the Middle East to match its own glorious past. They believe the West has played, and continues to play, an important part in that failure.

A LONG MEMORY

During the early stages of the Iran-Iraq war, Saddam Hussein announced that his country was fighting 'a second Qadisiya'. The first Qadisiya was an Arab victory over the Persians (now Iranians) in 636–637 CE, but Arabs throughout the Middle East recognized the name. The years of Arab glory have not been forgotten, despite the centuries of submission to other peoples.

Glossary

Arab nationalists followers of the idea that Arab interests can best be promoted through Arab unity, and possibly even the creation of a single Arab state

Ba'athist person who follows a set of ideas based on Arab unity and modernization that led to the creation of Ba'ath political parties in several countries, particularly Syria and Iraq

civil war war between different groups in the same country

civilians non-members of the armed forces

Cold War name given to the hostility that existed between the free enterprise capitalist world led by the USA and the communist world led by the Soviet Union

colonies countries or areas that are controlled politically by more powerful countries

communist describes a political and economic system that claims to put the interests of society as a whole above the interests of individuals

conservative describes a person or political group that likes to keep things as they are, and is resistant to change

Crusades series of European military attacks on the Muslim Middle East, starting in the 11th century and ending in the 14th century

Dark Ages period of economic and cultural decline in Europe, lasting from the 5th century CE to the 8th century CE

democracy political system in which governments are regularly elected by the people, or a country in which this system exists

dictator individual who rules unrestricted by others

diplomacy management of relations between states by peaceful means. Diplomats are the people whose job it is to work on relations with other countries.

Fatah Palestinian resistance group set up by Yasser Arafat and others in 1959

free enterprise organization of an economy where individuals rather than governments make the decisions about which goods and services are produced, and how they are bought and sold

Gaza Strip strip of land along the eastern Mediterranean coast. Ruled by Great Britain from 1918–1948, Egypt from 1949–1967, Israel from 1967–1994 and the Palestinian National Authority (in places) from 1994 to the present day.

guerrilla war war fought on one side by unofficial and irregular troops, who have to rely on surprise and movement in their campaigns against more powerful official forces

Hamas Islamic fundamentalist Palestinian resistance group set up in 1987

hijacking violent takeover, usually of a plane, ship or other means of transport

Holy Land region of the Middle East, now mostly in Israel, where events important to Judaism (the Jewish religion), Christianity and Islam are believed to have taken place

immigration people moving to a new country

intifada campaign of resistance to Israeli occupation of the West Bank and Gaza Strip. The first intifada began in late 1987, and ended in 1993. A second began in the autumn of 2000. In Arabic, intifada means 'uprising'.

Islamic fundamentalist someone who believes in strictly following the rules, or a particular interpretation of the rules, of Islam's holy book, the Qur'an

Islamic Jihad Islamic fundamentalist Palestinian resistance group set up in 1979

League of Nations international organization set up after World War I to help settle disputes between nations

left-wing in politics usually associated with policies that place the needs of the whole community above the short-term demands of the individual

liberate to set free

mandates permissions to rule

millennium a thousand years

modernize bring up to date by making use of the latest ideas and technology

nationalize to turn a privately-owned company or organization into a government-owned one

occupied territories territories taken over and administered against the wishes of the inhabitants. In Arab-Israeli history, the phrase usually refers to the Palestinian territories occupied by Israel after its victory in the 1967 Six Day War. This includes the Gaza Strip (which had been ruled by Egypt between 1948 and 1967), and the West Bank (which had been ruled by Jordan in the same period).

oil concession permission to drill for, and to extract, oil

partition dividing up

PFLP (Popular Front for the Liberation of Palestine) left-wing Palestinian resistance group that pioneered terrorist hijackings in the late 1960s

PLO (Palestine Liberation Organization) organization created in 1964 to bring together the many political and military groups fighting for a Palestinian state

Qur'an holy book of Islam

refugees people who, for various reasons, have been forced to leave their own countries

Renaissance period of European intellectual and artistic progress that began in Italy in the 14th century

revolution overthrow of the existing political order

right-wing in politics, generally used to describe people and policies that favour individual rights over those of the community, nationalism over internationalism and traditional values over radical change

secular unrelated to religion or religious identities

Security Council decision-making body at the United Nations. It consists of fifteen members,

five of them permanent (the USA, the UK, France, Russia and China).

Semitic a racial and language group that includes both Arabs and Jews

settlements in the occupied territories, Israeli communities established since 1967

Shi'ite Muslims smaller of two major Muslim groups, which originated in a dispute over who should lead all Muslims. There are large numbers of Shi'ite Muslims in Iran and Iraq.

strategic to do with the placing of military forces

Suez Canal Zone area of Egypt including the Suez Canal that the UK continued to administer after the rest of Egypt had been given independence

suicide bomber person who deliberately kills him or herself in an attempt to kill others

Sunni Muslims larger of two major Muslim groups, which originated in a dispute over who should lead all Muslims. Sunnis are the majority in most Arab nations, including Egypt, Syria and Saudi Arabia.

terrorist person who uses intimidation and violence against people for political reasons

United Nations (UN) international body set up in 1945 to promote peace and cooperation between countries

Versailles peace talks talks held after World War I to discuss the new post-war borders and other matters

veto power to prevent something

War on Terror worldwide campaign to eliminate terrorism that began in September 2001, after the terrorist attacks on the USA on the 11th of that month

West Bank hilly area west of the River Jordan approximately 112 kilometres (70 miles) long and 48 kilometres (30 miles) wide. Ruled by Great Britain between 1918–1948, Jordan between 1948–1967 and Israel from 1967 to the present day. Since 1994 there has been a significant transfer of power in the towns to the Palestinian National Authority.

Zionist person who campaigns for an independent Jewish state

Facts and Figures

EGYPT
Official date of independence:	1922
Capital:	Cairo
Population 1960:	25,922,000
Population 2005:	77,505,756
GDP per capita:	US$4200
Oil reserves:	2.7 billion barrels

Prominent leaders: Gamal Abdul Nasser (1954–1970), Anwar Sadat (1970–1981), Hosni Mubarak (1981–present day)

IRAN
Capital:	Tehran
Population 1960:	21,554,000
Population 2005:	68,017,860
GDP per capita:	US$7700
Oil reserves:	130.8 billion barrels

Prominent leaders: Reza Shah (1925–1941), Mohammed Reza Shah (1941–1979), Ayatollah Khomeini (1979–1989), Ayatollah Khamene'i (1989–present day)

IRAQ
Official date of independence:	1932
Capital:	Baghdad
Population 1960:	6,847,000
Population 2005:	26,074,906
GDP per capita:	US$3500
Oil reserves:	112.5 billion barrels

Prominent leaders: Abdul Karim Qassem (1958–1963), Saddam Hussein (1979–2003)

ISRAEL
Official date of independence:	1948
Capital:	Jerusalem
Population 1960:	2,114,000
Population 2005:	6,276,883 (of which 389,000 are living in Israeli-occupied territories)
GDP per capita:	US$20,800
Oil reserves:	none

Prominent leaders: David Ben Gurion (1948–1953, 1955–1963), Golda Meir (1969–1974), Menachem Begin (1977–1983), Ariel Sharon (2001–present day)

JORDAN
Official date of independence:	1946
Capital:	Amman
Population 1960:	844,000
Population 2005:	5,759,732
GDP per capita:	US$4500
Oil reserves:	445,000 barrels

Prominent leaders: King Hussein (1952–1999), King Abdullah II (1999–present day)

KUWAIT
Official date of independence:	1961
Capital:	Kuwait City
Population 1960:	278,000
Population 2005:	2,335,648
GDP per capita:	US$21,300
Oil reserves:	96.5 billion barrels

LEBANON
Official date of independence:	1943
Capital:	Beirut
Population 1960:	1,968,420
Population 2005:	3,826,018
GDP per capita:	US$5000
Oil reserves:	none

SAUDI ARABIA
Official date of independence:	1932
Capital:	Riyadh
Population 1960:	4,075,000
Population 2005:	26,417,599
GDP per capita:	US$12,000
Oil reserves:	261.7 billion barrels

Prominent leaders: King Ibn Saud (1932–1953), King Faisal (1964–1975)

SYRIA
Official date of independence:	1946
Capital:	Damascus
Population 1960:	4,561,000
Population 2005:	18,448,752
GDP per capita:	US$3400
Oil reserves:	2.5 billion barrels

Prominent leaders: Hafez al-Assad (1971–2000), Bashar al-Assad (2000–present day)

UNITED ARAB EMIRATES
Official date of independence:	1971
Capital:	Abu Dhabi
Population 1960:	90,000
Population 2005:	2,563,212
GDP per capita:	US$25,200
Oil reserves:	97.8 billion barrels

The comparative GDP per capita figures for the UK and the USA are US$29,600 and US$40,100.

The oil reserve figures are from a global total of 1 trillion barrels.

(*Sources:* CIA World Factbook, 2005; *World Bank. Population and GDP per capita figures for 2005 are 2004 estimates.*)

Timeline

8000 BCE	8000 BCE	First agricultural settlements	1900	
		First cities and invention of writing		1908 — First oil production in Middle East
				1914–1918 — World War I
				1917 — Balfour Declaration
				1918–1919 — Versailles peace talks
			1920	1922 — Egypt given partial independence
1000 BCE	975 BCE	Jewish state in Palestine		1925 — Reza Khan takes power in Iran (Reza Shah Pahlavi)
			1930	1932 — Iraq given independence
				1932 — Founding of Saudi Arabia
				1933 — Standard Oil given Saudi oil concession
				1936 — Egypt gains independence
500 BCE				1939–1945 — World War II
			1940	1941 — Mohammed Reza Pahlavi becomes Shah of Iran
	334–323 BCE	Alexander the Great conquers the Middle East		1945 — US President Roosevelt holds talks with King Ibn Saud of Saudi Arabia
				1947 — UN agrees Palestine partition plan
	ca 100 BCE – 600 CE	Roman Empire in the Middle East		1948 — State of Israel declared
0		Jews expelled from Palestine	1950	1948–1949 — First Arab-Israeli War
				1952 — Nationalist revolution in Egypt
				1953 — Mossadegh overthrown in Iran
				1956 — Suez Crisis and Second Arab-Israeli War (The Sinai War)
				1958 — Nationalist revolution in Iraq
			1960	1960 — Founding of OPEC
				1964 — Founding of PLO
500 CE	ca 450–800 CE	Dark Ages in Europe		1967 — Third Arab-Israeli War (June War, Six Day War). UN Resolution 242.
	ca 570–632 CE	Life of the Prophet Mohammed		1969–1970 — Egyptian 'War of Attrition' against Israel
	632–750 CE	Rapid expansion of Arab Empire	1970	1969–1972 — First Palestinian terrorist attacks
				1973 — Fourth Arab-Israeli War (October War, Yom Kippur War) First use of Arab 'oil weapon'
				1976–1990 — Civil war in Lebanon
				1978–1992 — Civil war in Afghanistan
1000 CE			1980	1979 — Islamic Revolution in Iran
	1096–1270	Crusades		1980–1988 — Iran-Iraq War
	1219–1260	Mongol invasions of Middle East		
	1301–1918	Ottoman Empire	1990	1990 — Iraqi invasion of Kuwait
1500 CE				1991 — The Gulf War
			2000	2001 — 11 September attacks on World Trade Center in New York
	1869	Opening of Suez Canal		2003 — USA and UK invade Iraq
1900 CE				
			2010	

51

Who's Who?

Arafat, Yasser (Abu Ammar) Born in 1929, died in 2004. Arafat claimed to have been born in Jerusalem, but spent much of his childhood and youth in the Egyptian capital, Cairo. He fought as a volunteer in the First Arab-Israeli War, and in 1959 was a co-founder of the Palestinian resistance group Fatah. In 1969 he was elected chairman of the PLO (Palestinian Liberation Organization). After moving the PLO Headquarters from Jordan to Lebanon, he led the Palestinian resistance to the Israeli invasion of that country in 1982. After signing a partial peace with Israel in 1993, he became president of the Palestinian National Authority. He was, however, unable to reach a lasting agreement with Israel before his death in 2004.

al-Assad, Hafez Born in 1930, died in 2000. Al-Assad served as his country's president from 1971 until his death in 2000. As leader of the Syrian Ba'ath Party, he tried to modernize and strengthen Syria with Soviet economic and military help. His regime allowed little opposition, and ruthlessly suppressed an Islamic fundamentalist uprising in 1979–1982. He led Syria to war against Israel in 1973. Unlike Egypt's President Sadat, however, he refused to make a separate peace in later years. A long-time opponent of Iraqi Ba'athist Saddam Hussein, he supported both Iran and the British-American-led coalitions in their wars against Iraq.

Begin, Menachem Born in 1913, died in 1992. Begin was born in Brest-Litovsk (then in Russia). He became an active Zionist in the 1930s, and eventually reached Palestine with the Polish Free Army in 1943. A year later he joined the Irgun Zvai Leumi Jewish resistance group, which conducted a terrorist campaign against the British and Palestinian Arabs until Israeli independence. Begin was leader of the parliamentary opposition from 1948–1977. As prime minister (1977–1983), he negotiated a peace treaty with President Sadat of Egypt. He was, however, completely opposed to the idea of an independent Palestinian state.

Ben Gurion, David Born in 1886, died in 1973. Ben Gurion was born in Poland, but emigrated to Palestine in 1906. In World War I, he served with the Jewish Legion, which fought alongside the British against the Turks. He was leader of the Jewish labour movement in Palestine from 1921–1933, and leader of the Labour Party from 1930. He cooperated with the British during World War II, and led the struggle against them in 1946–1948. He was prime minister of Israel from 1948–1953 and 1955–1963, and remained an influential figure right up to his death.

Bin Laden, Osama Born in 1957. Bin Laden was born in Saudi Arabia, the son of a rich construction company owner. He became an Islamic fundamentalist in his twenties, and travelled to Afghanistan to take part in the war against the Soviet occupation. With victory assured, he and other Islamic fundamentalists formed Al-Qaeda to fight wherever it was needed for the fundamentalist cause. In 2001 he masterminded the 11 September attacks on the USA, and has been the object of a worldwide manhunt ever since.

Hussein, Saddam Born in 1937. Hussein joined the Iraqi Ba'ath Party in 1957 and played a leading role in the 1968 coup that brought it to power. Vice-president and head of the national security services from 1969, he became president in 1979. At home, he pursued a policy of modernization, taking over the Iraqi oil industry and launching extensive development programmes. Abroad, he fought a costly war with Iran (1980–1988), and then tried to pay for it by taking over Kuwait. After being ejected by an international coalition, he refused to cooperate fully with the international community. Hussein was eventually overthrown by an invasion carried out mainly by the USA and the UK in 2003.

Ibn Saud (King Abdul Aziz Ibn Abdul Rahman Al Saud) Born ca 1880, died in 1953. Saud was born in the Arabian city of Riyadh. Exiled with his family by a rival tribe in 1890, he took back the city in 1902. Over the next 30 years, he gradually extended his hold over most of the Arabian Peninsula, founding the state of Saudi Arabia in 1932.

Khomeini, Ayatollah Born in 1902, died in 1989. Khomeini came to prominence as an Iranian Shi'ite religious leader. He was a bitter opponent of the Shah of Iran's pro-Western policies. Because of this, Khomeini was exiled in 1964, and spent fifteen years in Turkey, Iraq and France. After the overthrow of the Shah in 1979, he returned to lead the new Islamic Republic of Iran. He fought a defensive war against Iraq between 1980 and 1988. He gave help to fundamentalist groups in other Muslim countries, including Lebanon and Afghanistan.

Lawrence, T. E. ('Lawrence of Arabia') Born in 1888, died in 1935. Lawrence worked as an archaeologist in the Middle East before World War I, and served in Army intelligence during the war. In 1916 he was sent to help organize Arab military resistance to the Turks. He then played an active role in other anti-Turkish operations, particularly against the Hejaz Railway (which ran south from Jordan to Medina in Arabia). After the war he briefly served as an adviser on Arab affairs to the British government.

Mohammed Born ca 570 CE, died in 632 CE. The Prophet Mohammed was born in Mecca. According to his own testimony, he began, around the age of 40, to receive revelations from God. His written record of these became Islam's holy book, the Qur'an. Written records of Mohammed's sayings and daily behaviour became known, respectively, as the Hadith and Sunna. These, along with the Qur'an, form the sources of guidance for his Muslim followers. Forced to leave Mecca in 622, he then set up his religious community in Medina. In 630 he returned to Mecca as a conqueror. By the time of his death in 632, he controlled most of the Arabian Peninsula. Today, there are over one billion Muslims worldwide.

Mossadegh, Mohammed Born in 1882, died in 1967. Mossadegh was born in Tehran, in what is now Iran. Educated as a lawyer in Switzerland, he became Iranian prime minister in 1951. A passionate nationalist, he tried to nationalize the Iranian oil industry. Opposed by both the young pro-Western Shah of Iran and the Western oil companies, he was overthrown in 1953. Released from prison in 1956, Mossadegh was kept under house arrest until his death.

Nasser, Gamal Abdul Born in 1918, died in 1970. Nasser was a leading member of the Egyptian Free Officers who overthrew the government of King Farouk in 1952. He served as prime minister from 1954 to 1956 and president from 1956 to his death in 1970. Nasser was a committed Arab nationalist. He used Soviet help to strengthen the Egyptian economy and armed forces, and tried to create an United Arab Republic with Syria. After losing the 1967 war with Israel, he tried to resign, but huge demonstrations of support persuaded him to remain in office. Unlike most Arab leaders, his popularity extended throughout the Arab world.

Pahlavi, Mohammed Reza Shah Born in 1919, died in 1980. Pahlavi became Shah of Iran when his father Reza Shah Pahlavi gave up the throne in 1941. After the fall of Mohammed Mossadegh (see left) in 1953, he allied himself with the USA, and launched a programme of economic development and social reform. In the 1970s the failure of his economic policies and the heavy-handedness of his security police made him extremely unpopular. He was overthrown in 1979, and died the following year in Egypt.

Sadat, Anwar Born in 1918, died in 1981. Sadat was a prominent member of the Egyptian Free Officers who overthrew the government of King Farouk in 1952. He served as Nasser's vice-president between 1964 and 1966 and again between 1969 and 1970, and succeeded him as president in 1970. He started and lost the Third Arab-Israeli War in 1973. After the defeat he moved away from the Soviet Union and closer to the USA. He reached a separate peace agreement with Israel in 1978, and was assassinated by an Islamic fundamentalist in 1981.

Find Out More

BOOKS FOR YOUNGER READERS

One of the best resources on the Middle East for younger readers is the 'Middle East' series, of which this book is a part:

Iran and the Islamic Revolution, John King (Raintree, 2006)

Iraq Then and Now, John King (Raintree, 2006)

Israel and Palestine, John King (Raintree, 2006)

Oil in the Middle East, John King (Raintree, 2006)

Other useful books for younger readers include:

The Arab-Israeli Conflict (Troubled World Series), Ivan Minnis (Raintree, 2003)
Historical facts about the conflict between Israel and the Arabs presented in an approachable way.

Saddam Hussein and Iraq, David Downing (Raintree, 2003)
The story of Saddam's rise to power and his leadership of Iraq.

Yasser Arafat, David Downing (Raintree, 2002)
A biography of the Palestinian leader.

BOOKS FOR OLDER READERS

The Gun and the Olive Branch: The Roots of Violence in the Middle East, David Hirst (Faber & Faber, 2003)
A history of Arab-Jewish relations in Palestine.

The Middle East Since 1945, Stewart Ross (Teach Yourself, 2004)
An outline of post-war events.

A Peace to End All Peace: The Fall of the Ottoman Empire and the Creation of the Modern Middle East, David Fromkin (Avon, 1989)
A study of the Middle East in and after World War I.

Pity the Nation: Lebanon at War, Robert Fisk (Andre Deutsch, 1990)
An in-depth study of the civil war in Lebanon.

Sowing the Wind: The Seeds of Conflict in the Middle East, John Keay (John Murray, 2003)
A survey of Middle East history in the first half of the 20th century.

ADDRESSES TO WRITE TO

If you want to find out more about the history of the Middle East, try contacting these organizations:

IN THE UK

The London Middle East Institute
Room 479
School of Oriental and African Studies
University of London
Russell Square
London WC1H OXG

The Royal Institute of International Affairs
Chatham House
10 St James's Square
London SW1Y 4LE

International Institute for Strategic Studies
Arundel House
13–15 Arundel Street
Temple Place
London WC2R 3DX

IN AUSTRALIA

The Centre for Middle East and North African Studies
Macquarie University
Sydney 2109

The Centre for Middle Eastern and Central Asian Studies
Australian National University
Canberra ACT 0200

Index

Numbers in *italics* refer to captions to illustrations

Index

Titles in *The Middle East* series include:

Hardback   1-844-43206-8

Hardback   1-844-43205-X

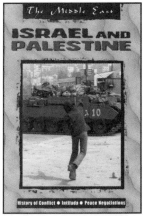

Hardback   1-844-43204-1

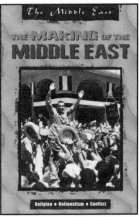

Hardback   1-844-43203-3

Hardback   1-844-43207-6

Find out about other titles from Raintree on our website www.raintreepublishers.co.uk